WHAT MAKES AN
EFFECTIVE EXECUTIVE

HARVARD BUSINESS REVIEW
CLASSICS

WHAT MAKES AN EFFECTIVE EXECUTIVE

Peter F. Drucker

Harvard Business Review Press
Boston, Massachusetts

Copyright 2017 Harvard Business School Publishing Corporation
Originally published in *Harvard Business Review* in June 2004
Reprint #R0406C
All rights reserved

Printed in the United States of America

10 9 8 7 6 5 4 3 2 1

ISBN: 978-1-63369-254-1
eISBN: 978-1-63369-255-8

THE HARVARD BUSINESS
REVIEW CLASSICS SERIES

Since 1922, *Harvard Business Review* has
been a leading source of breakthrough ideas
in management practice—many of which still
speak to and influence us today. The HBR
Classics series now offers you the opportunity
to make these seminal pieces a part of your
permanent management library. Each vol-
ume contains a groundbreaking idea that has
shaped best practices and inspired countless
managers around the world—and will change
how you think about the business world today.

WHAT MAKES AN EFFECTIVE EXECUTIVE

An effective executive does not need to be a leader in the sense that the term is now most commonly used. Harry Truman did not have one ounce of charisma, for example, yet he was among the most effective chief executives in U.S. history. Similarly, some of the best business and nonprofit CEOs I've worked with over a 65-year consulting career were not stereotypical leaders. They were all over the map in terms of their personalities, attitudes, values, strengths, and weaknesses. They ranged from extroverted to nearly reclusive, from easygoing to controlling, from generous to parsimonious.

What made them all effective is that they followed the same eight practices:

- They asked, "What needs to be done?"

- They asked, "What is right for the enterprise?"

- They developed action plans.

- They took responsibility for decisions.

- They took responsibility for communicating.

- They were focused on opportunities rather than problems.

- They ran productive meetings.

- They thought and said "we" rather than "I."

The first two practices gave them the knowledge they needed. The next four helped them convert this knowledge into effective action. The last two ensured that the whole organization felt responsible and accountable.

GET THE KNOWLEDGE YOU NEED

The first practice is to ask what needs to be done. Note that the question is not "What do I want to do?" Asking what has to be done, and taking the question seriously, is crucial for managerial success. Failure to ask this question will render even the ablest executive ineffectual.

When Truman became president in 1945, he knew exactly what he wanted to do: complete the economic and social reforms of Roosevelt's New Deal, which had been deferred by World War II. As soon as he asked what needed to be done, though, Truman realized that foreign affairs had absolute priority. He organized his working day so that it began with tutorials on foreign policy by the secretaries of state and defense. As a result, he became the most effective president in foreign affairs the United States has ever known. He contained Communism in both Europe and Asia and, with the Marshall Plan, triggered 50 years of world-wide economic growth.

Similarly, Jack Welch realized that what needed to be done at General Electric when he took over as chief executive was not the overseas expansion he wanted to launch. It was getting rid of GE businesses that, no matter how profitable, could not be number one or number two in their industries.

The answer to the question "What needs to be done?" almost always contains more than one urgent task. But effective executives do not splinter themselves. They concentrate on one task if at all possible. If they are among those people—a sizable minority—who work best with a change of pace in their working day, they pick two tasks. I have never encountered an executive who remains effective while tackling more than two tasks at a time. Hence, after asking what needs to be done, the effective executive sets priorities and sticks to them. For a CEO, the priority task might be redefining the company's mission. For a unit head, it might be redefining the unit's relationship with headquarters. Other tasks, no matter how important or appealing, are postponed. However, after completing the original top-priority task, the executive resets priorities rather than moving on to number two from the original list. He asks, "What must be done now?" This generally results in new and different priorities.

To refer again to America's best-known CEO: Every five years, according to his autobiography, Jack Welch asked himself, "What needs to be done *now*?" And every time, he came up with a new and different priority.

But Welch also thought through another issue before deciding where to concentrate his efforts for the next five years. He asked himself which of the two or three tasks at the top of the list he himself was best suited to undertake. Then he concentrated on that task; the others he delegated. Effective executives try to focus on jobs they'll do especially well. They know that enterprises perform if top management performs—and don't if it doesn't.

Effective executives' second practice—fully as important as the first—is to ask, "Is this the right thing for the enterprise?" They do not ask if it's right for the owners, the stock price, the employees, or the executives. Of course they know that shareholders, employees, and executives are important constituencies who have to support a decision, or at least acquiesce in it, if the choice is to be effective. They know that the share price is important not only for the shareholders but also for the enterprise, since the price/earnings ratio sets the cost of capital. But they also know that a decision that isn't right for the enterprise will ultimately not be right for any of the stakeholders.

This second practice is especially important for executives at family owned or family run businesses—the majority of businesses in every country—particularly when they're making decisions about people. In the successful family company, a relative is promoted only if he or she is measurably superior to all nonrelatives on the same level. At DuPont, for instance, all top managers (except the controller and lawyer) were family members in the early years when the firm was run as a family business. All male descendants of the founders were entitled to entry-level jobs at the company. Beyond the entrance level, a family member got a promotion only if a panel composed primarily of nonfamily managers judged the person to be superior in ability and performance to all other employees at the same level. The same rule was observed for a century in the highly successful British family business J. Lyons & Company (now part of a major conglomerate) when it dominated the British food-service and hotel industries.

Asking "What is right for the enterprise?" does not guarantee that the right decision will be made. Even the most brilliant executive is human and thus prone to mistakes and prejudices. But failure to ask the question virtually guarantees the *wrong* decision.

WRITE AN ACTION PLAN

Executives are doers; they execute. Knowledge is useless to executives until it has been translated into deeds. But before springing into action, the executive needs to plan his course. He needs to think about desired results, probable restraints, future revisions, check-in points, and implications for how he'll spend his time.

First, the executive defines desired results by asking: "What contributions should the enterprise expect from me over the next 18 months to two years? What results will I commit to? With what deadlines?" Then he considers the restraints on action: "Is this course of action ethical? Is it acceptable within the organization? Is it legal? Is it compatible with the mission, values, and policies of the organization?" Affirmative answers don't guarantee that the action will be effective. But violating these restraints is certain to make it both wrong and ineffectual.

The action plan is a statement of intentions rather than a commitment. It must not become a straitjacket. It should be revised often, because every success creates new opportunities. So does every failure. The same is true for changes in the business environment, in the market, and especially in people within the enterprise—all these changes demand that the plan be revised. A written plan should anticipate the need for flexibility.

In addition, the action plan needs to create a system for checking the results against the expectations. Effective executives usually build two such checks into their action plans. The first check comes halfway through the plan's time period; for example, at nine months. The second occurs at the end, before the next action plan is drawn up.

Finally, the action plan has to become the basis for the executive's time management.

Time is an executive's scarcest and most precious resource. And organizations— whether government agencies, businesses, or nonprofits—are inherently time wasters. The action plan will prove useless unless it's allowed to determine how the executive spends his or her time.

Napoleon allegedly said that no successful battle ever followed its plan. Yet Napoleon also planned every one of his battles, far more meticulously than any earlier general had done. Without an action plan, the executive becomes a prisoner of events. And without check-ins to reexamine the plan as events unfold, the executive has no way of knowing which events really matter and which are only noise.

ACT

When they translate plans into action, executives need to pay particular attention to decision making, communication, opportunities (as opposed to problems), and meetings. I'll consider these one at a time.

Take Responsibility for Decisions

A decision has not been made until people know:

- the name of the person accountable for carrying it out;

- the deadline;

- the names of the people who will be affected by the decision and therefore have to know about, understand, and approve it—or at least not be strongly opposed to it—and

- the names of the people who have to be informed of the decision, even if they are not directly affected by it.

An extraordinary number of organizational decisions run into trouble because these bases aren't covered. One of my clients, 30 years ago, lost its leadership position in the fast-growing Japanese market because the company, after deciding to enter into a joint venture with a new Japanese partner, never made clear who was to inform the purchasing agents that the partner defined its specifications in meters and kilograms rather than feet and pounds—and nobody ever did relay that information.

It's just as important to review decisions periodically—at a time that's been agreed on in advance—as it is to make them carefully in the first place. That way, a poor decision can be corrected before it does real damage. These reviews can cover anything from the results to the assumptions underlying the decision.

Such a review is especially important for the most crucial and most difficult of all decisions, the ones about hiring or promoting people. Studies of decisions about people show that only one-third of such choices turn out to be truly successful. One-third are likely to be draws—neither successes nor outright failures. And one-third are failures, pure and simple. Effective executives know this and check-up (six to nine months later) on the results of their people decisions. If they find that a decision has not had the desired results, they don't conclude that the person has not performed. They conclude, instead, that they themselves made a mistake. In a well-managed enterprise, it is understood that people who fail in a new job, especially after a promotion, may not be the ones to blame.

Executives also owe it to the organization and to their fellow workers not to tolerate nonperforming individuals in important jobs. It may not be the employees' fault that they are underperforming, but even so, they have to be removed. People who have failed in a new job should be given the choice to go

back to a job at their former level and salary.
This option is rarely exercised; such people,
as a rule, leave voluntarily, at least when
their employers are U.S. firms. But the very
existence of the option can have a powerful
effect, encouraging people to leave safe,
comfortable jobs and take risky new assignments. The organization's performance
depends on employees' willingness to take
such chances.

A systematic decision review can be a
powerful tool for self-development, too.
Checking the results of a decision against
its expectations shows executives what their
strengths are, where they need to improve,
and where they lack knowledge or information. It shows them their biases. Very often

it shows them that their decisions didn't produce results because they didn't put the right people on the job. Allocating the best people to the right positions is a crucial, tough job that many executives slight, in part because the best people are already too busy. Systematic decision review also shows executives their own weaknesses, particularly the areas in which they are simply incompetent. In these areas, smart executives don't make decisions or take actions. They delegate. Everyone has such areas; there's no such thing as a universal executive genius.

Most discussions of decision making assume that only senior executives make decisions or that only senior

executives' decisions matter. This is
a dangerous mistake. Decisions are
made at every level of the organization,
beginning with individual professional
contributors and frontline supervisors.
These apparently low-level decisions
are extremely important in a knowledge-
based organization. Knowledge workers
are supposed to know more about their
areas of specialization—for example, tax
accounting—than anybody else, so their
decisions are likely to have an impact
throughout the company. Making good
decisions is a crucial skill at every level.
It needs to be taught explicitly to everyone
in organizations that are based on
knowledge.

Take Responsibility for Communicating

Effective executives make sure that both their action plans and their information needs are understood. Specifically, this means that they share their plans with and ask for comments from all their colleagues—superiors, subordinates, and peers. At the same time, they let each person know what information they'll need to get the job done. The information flow from subordinate to boss is usually what gets the most attention. But executives need to pay equal attention to peers' and superiors' information needs.

We all know, thanks to Chester Barnard's 1938 classic *The Functions of the Executive*, that organizations are held together by information rather than by ownership or command. Still, far too many executives behave as if information and its flow were the job of the information specialist—for example, the accountant. As a result, they get an enormous amount of data they do not need and cannot use, but little of the information they do need. The best way around this problem is for each executive to identify the information he needs, ask for it, and keep pushing until he gets it.

Focus on Opportunities

Good executives focus on opportunities rather than problems. Problems have to be taken care of, of course; they must not be swept under the rug. But problem solving, however necessary, does not produce results. It prevents damage. Exploiting opportunities produces results.

Above all, effective executives treat change as an opportunity rather than a threat. They systematically look at changes, inside and outside the corporation, and ask, "How can we exploit this change as an opportunity for our enterprise?" Specifically, executives scan these seven situations for opportunities:

- an unexpected success or failure in their own enterprise, in a competing enterprise, or in the industry;

- a gap between what is and what could be in a market, process, product, or service (for example, in the nineteenth century, the paper industry concentrated on the 10% of each tree that became wood pulp and totally neglected the possibilities in the remaining 90%, which became waste);

- innovation in a process, product, or service, whether inside or outside the enterprise or its industry;

- changes in industry structure and market structure;

- demographics;

- changes in mind-set, values, perception, mood, or meaning; and

- new knowledge or a new technology.

Effective executives also make sure that problems do not overwhelm opportunities.

In most companies, the first page of the monthly management report lists key problems. It's far wiser to list opportunities on the first page and leave problems for the second page. Unless there is a true catastrophe, problems are not discussed in management meetings until opportunities have been analyzed and properly dealt with.

Staffing is another important aspect of being opportunity focused. Effective executives put their best people on opportunities rather than on problems. One way to staff for opportunities is to ask each member of the management group to prepare two lists every six months—a list of opportunities for the entire enterprise and a list of the best-performing people throughout the enterprise. These are discussed, then melded into two master lists, and the best people are matched with the best opportunities. In Japan, by the way, this matchup is considered a major HR task in a big corporation or government department; that practice is one of the key strengths of Japanese business.

Make Meetings Productive

The most visible, powerful, and, arguably, effective nongovernmental executive in the America of World War II and the years thereafter was not a businessman. It was Francis Cardinal Spellman, the head of the Roman Catholic Archdiocese of New York and adviser to several U.S. presidents. When Spellman took over, the diocese was bankrupt and totally demoralized. His successor inherited the leadership position in the American Catholic church. Spellman often said that during his waking hours he was alone only twice each day, for 25 minutes each time: when he said Mass in his private chapel after getting up in the morning and when he said his evening prayers before going to bed. Otherwise he was always with people in a meeting, starting at breakfast with one Catholic organization and ending at dinner with another.

Top executives aren't quite as imprisoned as the archbishop of a major Catholic diocese. But every study of the executive workday has found that even junior executives and professionals are with other people—that is,

in a meeting of some sort—more than half of
every business day. The only exceptions are
a few senior researchers. Even a conversa-
tion with only one other person is a meeting.
Hence, if they are to be effective, executives
must make meetings productive. They must
make sure that meetings are work sessions
rather than bull sessions.

The key to running an effective meeting is
to decide in advance what kind of meeting it
will be. Different kinds of meetings require
different forms of preparation and different
results:

- *A meeting to prepare a statement, an
  announcement, or a press release.* For
  this to be productive, one member has

to prepare a draft beforehand. At the
meeting's end, a preappointed member
has to take responsibility for dissemi-
nating the final text.

- *A meeting to make an announcement—*
  for example, an organizational change.
  This meeting should be confined to
  the announcement and a discussion
  about it.

- *A meeting in which one member*
  reports. Nothing but the report should
  be discussed.

- *A meeting in which several or all mem-*
  bers report. Either there should be
  no discussion at all or the discussion

should be limited to questions for clarification. Alternatively, for each report there could be a short discussion in which all participants may ask questions. If this is the format, the reports should be distributed to all participants well before the meeting. At this kind of meeting, each report should be limited to a preset time—for example, 15 minutes.

- *A meeting to inform the convening executive.* The executive should listen and ask questions. He or she should sum up but not make a presentation.

- *A meeting whose only function is to allow the participants to be in*

the executive's presence. Cardinal
Spellman's breakfast and dinner meetings were of that kind. There is no way
to make these meetings productive.
They are the penalties of rank. Senior
executives are effective to the extent to
which they can prevent such meetings
from encroaching on their workdays.
Spellman, for instance, was effective
in large part because he confined such
meetings to breakfast and dinner and
kept the rest of his working day free
of them.

Making a meeting productive takes a
good deal of self-discipline. It requires that
executives determine what kind of meeting

is appropriate and then stick to that format. It's also necessary to terminate the meeting as soon as its specific purpose has been accomplished. Good executives don't raise another matter for discussion. They sum up and adjourn.

Good follow-up is just as important as the meeting itself. The great master of follow-up was Alfred Sloan, the most effective business executive I have ever known. Sloan, who headed General Motors from the 1920s until the 1950s, spent most of his six working days a week in meetings—three days a week in formal committee meetings with a set membership, the other three days in ad hoc meetings with individual GM executives or with a small group of executives. At the beginning of a formal meeting, Sloan announced the meeting's purpose. He then listened. He never took notes and he rarely spoke except to clarify a confusing point. At the end he summed up, thanked the participants, and left.

Then he immediately wrote a short memo addressed to one attendee of the meeting. In that note, he summarized the discussion and its conclusions and spelled out any work assignment decided upon in the meeting (including a decision to hold another meeting on the subject or to study an issue). He specified the deadline and the executive who was to be accountable for the assignment. He sent a copy of the memo to everyone who'd been present at the meeting. It was through these memos—each a small masterpiece—that Sloan made himself into an outstandingly effective executive.

Effective executives know that any given meeting is either productive or a total waste of time.

THINK AND SAY "WE"

The final practice is this: Don't think or say "I." Think and say "we." Effective executives know that they have ultimate responsibility, which can be neither shared nor delegated. But they have authority only because they have the trust of the organization. This means that they think of the needs and the opportunities of the organization before they think of their own needs and opportunities. This one may sound simple; it isn't, but it needs to be strictly observed.

We've just reviewed eight practices of effective executives. I'm going to throw in one final, bonus practice. This one's so important that I'll elevate it to the level of a rule: Listen first, speak last.

Effective executives differ widely in their personalities, strengths, weaknesses, values, and beliefs. All they have in common is that they get the right things done. Some are born effective. But the demand is much too great to be satisfied by extraordinary talent. Effectiveness is a discipline. And, like every discipline, effectiveness can be learned and must be earned.

ABOUT THE AUTHOR

Peter F. Drucker was a writer, consultant, and professor of social science and management at Claremont Graduate University in California. His thirty-nine books have been published in more than seventy languages. He founded the Peter F. Drucker Foundation for Nonprofit Management, and counseled thirteen governments, public services institutions, and major corporations.

ALSO BY THIS AUTHOR

Harvard Business Review Press Books

The Changing World of the Executive

*Classic Drucker: Essential Wisdom
of Peter Drucker from the Pages of
Harvard Business Review*

*The Frontiers of Management: Where
Tomorrow's Ideas Are Being Shaped
Today*

Managing in a Time of Great Change

Men, Ideas, and Politics

Managing Oneself

People and Performance: The Best of Peter Drucker on Management

Peter Drucker on the Profession of Management

The Peter F. Drucker Reader

The Theory of the Business

Technology, Management, and Society

Toward the Next Economics, and Other Essays

Harvard Business Review **Articles**

"The Coming of the New Organization"

"The Discipline of Innovation"

"The Effective Decision"

"How to Make People Decisions"

"Managing for Business Effectiveness"

"Managing Oneself"

"New Templates for Today's Organizations"

"The Theory of the Business"

"They're Not Employees, They're People"

Article Summary

Idea in Brief

Worried that you're not a born leader? That you lack charisma, the right talents, or some other secret ingredient? No need: leadership isn't about personality or talent. In fact, the best leaders exhibit wildly different personalities, attitudes, values, and strengths—they're extroverted or reclusive, easygoing or controlling, generous or parsimonious, numbers or vision oriented.

So what do effective leaders have in common?
They get the right things done, in the right ways—
by following eight simple rules:

- Ask what needs to be done.

- Ask what's right for the enterprise.

- Develop action plans.

- Take responsibility for decisions.

- Take responsibility for communicating.

- Focus on opportunities, not problems.

- Run productive meetings.

- Think and say "We," not "I."

Using discipline to apply these rules, you
gain the knowledge you need to make smart
decisions, convert that knowledge into effective
action, and ensure accountability throughout your
organization.

Idea in Practice

Get the Knowledge You Need

- **Ask what needs to be done.** When Jack Welch asked this question while taking over as CEO at General Electric, he realized that dropping GE businesses that couldn't be first or second in their industries was essential— not the overseas expansion he had wanted to launch. Once you know what must be done, identify tasks you're best at, concentrating on one at a time. After completing a task, reset priorities based on new realities.

- **Ask what's right for the enterprise.** Don't agonize over what's best for owners, investors, employees, or customers. Decisions that are right for your enterprise are ultimately right for all stakeholders.

Convert Your Knowledge into Action

- **Develop action plans.** Devise plans that
  specify desired results and constraints (is
  the course of action legal and compatible
  with the company's mission, values, and
  policies?). Include check-in points and implications for how you'll spend your time. And
  revise plans to reflect new opportunities.

- **Take responsibility for decisions.** Ensure
  that each decision specifies who's accountable for carrying it out, when it must be
  implemented, who'll be affected by it, and
  who must be informed. Regularly review
  decisions, especially hires and promotions.
  This enables you to correct poor decisions
  before doing real damage.

Take Responsibility for Communicating

- **Get input from superiors, subordinates, and peers on your action plans.** Let each know what information you need to get the job done. Pay equal attention to peers' and superiors' information needs.

- **Focus on opportunities, not problems.** You get results by exploiting opportunities, not solving problems. Identify changes inside and outside your organization (new technologies, product innovations, new market structures), asking "How can we exploit this change to benefit our enterprise?" Then match your best people with the best opportunities.

Ensure Companywide Accountability

- **Run productive meetings.** Articulate each meeting's purpose (Making an announcement? Delivering a report?). Terminate the meeting once the purpose is accomplished. Follow up with short communications summarizing the discussion, spelling out new work assignments and deadlines for completing them. General Motors CEO Alfred Sloan's legendary mastery of meeting follow-up helped secure GM's industry dominance in the mid-twentieth century.

- **Think and say "We," not "I."** Your authority comes from your organization's trust in you. To get the best results, always consider your organization's needs and opportunities before your own.

The most important management ideas all in one place.

We hope you enjoyed this book from *Harvard Business Review*. For the best ideas HBR has to offer turn to HBR's 10 Must Reads Boxed Set. From books on leadership and strategy to managing yourself and others, this 6-book collection delivers articles on the most essential business topics to help you succeed.

HBR's 10 Must Reads Series

The definitive collection of ideas and best practices on our most sought-after topics from the best minds in business.

- Change Management
- Collaboration
- Communication
- Emotional Intelligence
- Innovation
- Leadership
- Making Smart Decisions

- Managing Across Cultures
- Managing People
- Managing Yourself
- Strategic Marketing
- Strategy
- Teams
- The Essentials

hbr.org/mustreads

Buy for your team, clients, or event.
Visit hbr.org/bulksales for quantity discount rates.